Hope you enjoy the book!

Sincerely,

value

These quotations were gathered lovingly but unscientifically over several years and/or contributed by many friends or acquaintances. Some arrived, and survived in our files, on scraps of paper and may therefore be imperfectly worded or attributed. To the authors, contributors and original sources, our thanks, and where appropriate, our apologies.—The editors

CREDITS

Compiled by Kobi Yamada
Designed by Steve Potter

ISBN: 1-932319-42-5

 Contact: Compendium, Inc., 600 North 36th Street, Suite 400, Seattle, WA 98103. This book may be ordered directly from the publisher, but please try your local bookstore first. Call us at 800-91-IDEAS or come see our full line of inspiring products at www.compendiuminc.com.

Printed in China

Excellence isn't our goal.
It's where we begin.

KELLOGG SLOGAN

THE LURE
OF QUANTITY
IS THE MOST
DANGEROUS
OF ALL.

SIMONE WEIL

Better brands.
Best brands.
I don't believe
bigger is better.
I believe
better is better.
Period.

LESLIE H. WEXNER

Which is more important—
great quality or great service?
The answer is neither.
The objective is customer Value—
the overall combination of things,
people and experiences that creates
a total customer perception
of value received.

KARL ALBRECHT

Value is not any single thing, it's an aura, an atmosphere, an overpowering feeling that a company is doing everything with excellence.

JACK WELCH

A FIRST-RATE SOUP IS MORE CREATIVE
THAN A SECOND-RATE PAINTING.

ABRAHAM MASLOW

No matter what business we're in, the goal is quality and the challenge is reaching it.

FRED SMITH, FEDERAL EXPRESS

When true value is created,

the whole world profits—

not just your company,

but your customer.

SCOTT JOHNSON, SUN MICROSYSTEMS

THE VALUE
OF A SERVICE OR PRODUCT
IS NOT WHAT YOU PUT INTO IT—
IT IS WHAT YOUR
CUSTOMER
GETS OUT OF IT.
IF YOUR CUSTOMER PROFITS,
YOU PROFIT.

PETER DRUCKER

THE MARK OF A TRUE PROFESSIONAL
IS GIVING MORE THAN YOU GET.

ROBERT KIRBY

A company that makes
nothing but money is
a poor company.
To succeed, try to see
how much you can give
for a dollar, instead of
how little you can give
for a dollar.

HENRY FORD

Giving people a little more than they expect is a good way to get back a lot more than you'd expect.

ROBERT HALF

The principle was right there—

you couldn't miss it.

The more we did

for our customers,

the more they did for us.

DEBBI FIELDS

Careful! It's human nature to confuse "bigger" and "more" with "better." In the long run, the quantity of your transactions is not nearly as important as the quality of your relationships.

DAN ZADRA

There are three things

that are important

at Starbucks.

Relationships is the first,

and the other two

don't matter.

LINDA THOMPSON, STARBUCKS

Customers can smell emotional commitment a mile away. Every single person in the entire organization needs to speak the language of quality, service and value very fluently.

TOM PETERS

Be everywhere, do every-thing, and never fail to astonish the customer.

MACY'S SLOGAN

All of us
are the company,
and each of us
must be committed
to providing
superior value and
personalized service
every single time
to our customers.

JAY MEDICA

Creating value for our customers doesn't just happen—it comes from spunk, energy, constant chatter, collaboration with our customers and imagination.

TOM PETERS

LEFT TO OUR OWN DEVICES, WE TYPICALLY PAY MORE AND MORE ATTENTION TO THINGS OF LESS AND LESS IMPORTANCE TO OUR CUSTOMER.

RON ZEMKE

We shouldn't try to fit our customers into what we think they want. Ask them, and they will tell ya!

TOM PICKETT

The quality of any product or service
is what the customer says it is.

TECHSONIC

Customers perceive service and value in their own unique, idiosyncratic, emotional, irrational, end-of-the-day, and totally human terms. Perception is all there is!

TOM PETERS

Throughout the company, we are no longer measuring results against our expectations because our opinions don't count. They are irrelevant. It's only the customers' expectations that matter.

RICHARD C. NOTEBAERT, AMERITECH

THE MARKET NEVER
BOUGHT ANYTHING...PEOPLE DO.

UNKNOWN

THE DOLLAR BILLS
THE CUSTOMER GETS
FROM THE TELLER
IN FOUR BANKS
ARE THE SAME.
WHAT IS DIFFERENT
ARE THE TELLERS.

STANLEY MARCUS

Today, all restaurants are clean, all gas stations are convenient, all realtors have listings, and all banks have money. All things being equal, the distinguishing value now becomes your people.

PEOPLE BUY FROM THE PEOPLE THEY LIKE.

IBM SLOGAN

Hiring big-hearted people who sincerely love working with our customers is not just part of our value package, it's part of our brand.

CAROL GLOVER, BLUE PACIFIC

ALL SUCCESSFUL EMPLOYERS ARE STALKING PEOPLE WHO WILL DO THE UNUSUAL: PEOPLE WHO THINK, PEOPLE WHO CARE, PEOPLE WHO ATTRACT ATTENTION BY PERFORMING MORE THAN IS EXPECTED OF THEM.

DAVID J. SCHWARTZ

When you

can't afford to hire the best,

hire the young who are

going to be the best.

GERALDINE STUTZ

Ye shall be
known by
the quality
and vitality
of your
company
spirit.

UNKNOWN

Better quality + lesser price =

value + spiritual attitude of

our employees = unbeatable.

HERB KELLEHER, SOUTHWEST AIRLINES

MEDIOCRITY IS THE ENEMY.

DON GALER

Mediocrity is the place in the middle; it's the best of the worst, or the worst of the best—and who really wants to live or work in a place like that?

DAN ZADRA

QUALITY IS A PROUD AND SOARING THING.

JESSICA JULIAN

If you don't
do it excellently,
don't do it at all.
Because if
it's not excellent,
it won't be profitable
or fun, and
if you're not in
business for fun
or profit, what are
you doing there?

ROBERT TOWNSEND

IT COSTS A LOT TO BUILD
A BAD PRODUCT.

NORMAN AUGUSTINE

Quality is not only right, it's free. And it is not only free, it is the most profitable product line we have.

HAROLD GENEEN

REPUTATIONS ARE MADE BY SEARCHING FOR THINGS THAT CAN'T BE DONE AND DOING THEM.

HARRY GREY

Don't just create
what the market
needs or wants.
Create what it
would love!

JOSH ARMSTRONG

EVERY PROJECT
WE TAKE ON STARTS WITH
A QUESTION:
HOW CAN WE DO
WHAT'S NEVER BEEN DONE
BEFORE?

POLLY BABARRE

I NEVER THINK ABOUT WHY SOMETHING HASN'T BEEN DONE ALREADY, BUT WHY NOBODY HAS DONE IT RIGHT YET.

MARCIA KILGORE

NEVER LEAVE WELL ENOUGH ALONE.

RAYMOND LOEWY, DESIGNER

I have an almost complete disregard of precedent and a faith in the possibility of something better. It irritates me to be told how things always have been done. I defy the tyranny of precedent. I cannot afford the luxury of a closed mind. I go for anything new that might improve the past.

CLARA BARTON

THERE IS NO PENALTY FOR OVERACHIEVEMENT.

GEORGE W. MILLER

PROMISE
A LOT AND
GIVE
EVEN MORE.

ANYTHONY J. D'ANGELO

IT'S BETTER TO HAVE THE PHILOSOPHY TO OUT-THINK YOUR COMPETITION THAN OUTSPEND THEM.

LES WOLFF

The trick for any sensible company is to keep topping itself—so that any "stolen" secrets are secrets to yesterday's success.

TOM PETERS, THE PURSUIT OF WOW

It is the service we are not obliged to give that people value the most.

JAMES C. PENNEY

Everything extra
that we voluntarily
give to our customers
comes back to us in
terms of reputation, loyalty
and referrals. It not only
feels good to surprise
and pamper our customers,
it's just smart business.

MICHAEL NOLAN

EMPOWER YOUR EMPLOYEES.
ELIMINATE BUREAUCRACY.
ROMANCE YOUR CUSTOMERS.
NO EXCEPTIONS,
NO EXCUSES.

JIM WILLIAMSON

If you're not romancing your customer, be very concerned about who is.

JAMES P. CECIL

Profit in business comes from repeat customers, customers who boast about your product or service in a way that brings friends with them.

W. EDWARDS DEMING

Two things in this world are true: People want what they don't have, and people have what they don't want. If you can find a way to connect those who have with those who want, you can provide enormous value and get very rich in the process.

KIM WRIGHT WILEY, E-BAY

OUR CUSTOMERS WILL BEGIN TO REALIZE THAT THEY REALLY CAN COUNT ON FASTER, CRISPER, MORE CARING AND PERSONAL SERVICE FROM US. THAT SPECIAL RELATIONSHIP TRANSLATES INTO REAL VALUE FOR OUR CUSTOMERS, AND WHEN OUR CUSTOMER WINS, WE WIN.

RON KENDRICK

If we are committed to creating value, and if we aren't afraid of the hard times, obstacles become utterly unimportant—and we're on our way.

CANDICE CARPENTER

Celebrating the joy of living fully.

Also available are these spirited companion books in The Good Life series of great quotations:

drive
friend
heart
hero
joy
moxie
service
spirit
success
thanks
vision
welcome
yes!